I0391051

GROUNDWORK

The Foundation for an *Unshakable* Brand

Benjamin E. Warsinske

BrandedWorld.co, Inc.

To all the creative entrepreneurs
who want to positively impact the world,
this book is for you.

Contents

Introduction

Have you felt it lately?

That lost feeling you might get when you look at a customer and know that there's something more they need, something more they are missing from your product. Do you feel like there's an unnamed expectation that you can't seem to fulfill?

There seems to be a new breed of consumer: A customer who appears to be sophisticated, savvy, and well researched. This new breed of consumer doesn't just want a product or service; they want something more, something bigger and something beyond a tangible product they can hold.

They want an experience.

Something intangible that connects them to the brand and immerses them into another world each time they interact with them. I'm going to teach you how to give it to them.

The Shift to Experiences

Brand experiences are becoming more intelligent and personalized, blending the physical and digital to create something truly unique for the customer. When thoughtfully designed, brand experiences increase the overall perception of the brand, evoke emotions, and deliver consistent, reliable results.

A few months ago, I stumbled upon an ad for Omni Resorts while flipping through a magazine. The ad read, *"Experiences are the most valuable currency."* This quote stuck with me. It captured an evident, perceivable shift that is happening across different markets: Consumers are becoming more refined and expect a seamless, technologically friendly experience, no matter which brand they are interacting with.

Services that once required a large staff to perform and execute tasks are being transformed into experiential applications on mobile devices. In-store experiences are shifting to become showrooms, where the customer browses the merchandize, then makes a purchase online.

In the restaurant space, kiosks and mobile apps are being launched in order to provide a more personalized and transparent customer experience.

Starbucks is a terrific example of a company who has embraced technology to enhance the experience they offer their customers.

The *Starbucks* mobile app allows customers to order in advance, see the curated music being played from the Spotify playlist, and see progress towards their next reward.

For me, this was a game changer. Not one to like to wait in line, I fully immersed myself into Starbucks' world. I would check my status, order my favorite hand crafted drink (grande double-dirty chai latte), and find new music from the curated playlists.

After months of participating in this new *Starbucks* experience, I recognized the combination of elements the company was creating to immerse me into a fully physical and digital world.

This close communication is achieved by studying brand intimacy levels. *MBLM*, a brand strategy and research firm, released a study on brand intimacy in 2015.

The study states, *"Through advances in neuroscience and psychology, we now have a better understanding of the decision-making process. We now know emotion is the driver of decisions, and our rational minds retrofit the selection after the fact. Furthermore, behavioral science suggests how we feel about a brand is the best predictor of behavior. "*

On a deeper level, experiences amplify and personify the core beliefs of the brand. It is why some customers immediately get attracted to certain brands or why they are the first to defend the brand and its actions or choices.

This close relationship between the customer and brand is not a coincidence but is intentionally designed. *MBLM*'s research has revealed that "the higher percentage of fusing customers a brand has, the greater propensity consumers have to pay more for its products."

MBLM describes this process as a sort of fusion – merging the customer and brand to form a mutual realization and expression.
The brand experience is continually shifting towards one of seamless integration between

real life interactions, augmented reality, and use of technology. It's already begun to infiltrate our daily view of communication via notifications, email, and messaging applications.

The One Consistent Component Across Unshakable Brands

No matter how fanciful or magical a brand experience is, there is a consistent foundation that forms unshakable brands.

This foundation stems not from the colors, flashy design, or catchy tag lines – but instead from a place that all organizations must focus on. I call it *GroundWork* – the process of forming the basis of why an organization exists, what its purpose is, how the mission will guide it forward, what the brand stands for and believes in, and what the principles are by which the brand will live and die.

To develop amazing brand experiences like *Disney* and *Starbucks* deliver on a consistent basis, we must first understand and unpack what a brand stands for and believes in. It is these often overlooked elements that are the driving force behind unshakable brands.

How does a brand get to this level of intimacy with its customers? How can a brand develop a designed experience that consistently performs and leaves the customer wanting more, further extending the experience across different platforms and media channels?

To understand how these exemplary brands are formed, we need to understand what they are not.

I will show you how to lay the *GroundWork* in order to make your brand truly *unshakable.*

Chapter 1:

Four Myths Surrounding Brands

I've worked for several companies, multi-national corporations and small, hyper-local organizations. I've experienced the struggle of working for companies that didn't know exactly who they are and what they stand for.

While working in one of these groups, the company decided they were going to rebrand. We went through weeks of strenuous effort and decision-making, only to come out in the end with freshly painted office walls, a new letterhead, and the exact same company as before.

No one addressed the core issues. When the rebranding was complete, the organization had a new look and feel, yet still operated in a dysfunctional way.

The organization had thrown their resources into the very myths you'll read in this chapter. They tried to develop a brand that they thought would be unshakable from the surface level, rather than addressing the root cause. I'd imagine they are still struggling to figure out just what their purpose is, what they stand for, and the principles that guide them.

Now, in my work as a brand strategist and business operations consultant, I've continued to come across these four myths of branding. Let's look at each and discuss them individually.

You'll quickly see why each myth is capable of hurting your brand more than helping it. Take notes of what not to do. It is time to put these myths to rest once and for all.

Myth 1: The first step of branding is to create logos, fonts, colors, and packaging

No! Branding is first and foremost **not** about the elements that you see and interact with. They are the surface of the brand. This is similar to saying that the first step to making a fast car is to paint it red. Brand strategy goes much deeper than what you see on the surface.

If you remember the story I regaled earlier, I mentioned that the company I'd previously been employed with undertook a major rebranding effort.

They focused on the surface level but found their way back to old habits fairly soon after the first initiative to rebrand.

If you were to invest in developing a brand identity only to have it fade back to what you were trying to let go of, how devastating would that be to your brand?

How would your brand be perceived? Would your audience lose trust in you? Would your team members and employees lose trust in the brand?

Myth 2: A designer or ad agency will create a brand for you

Nope. The idea that you can simply outsource your brand is simply untrue.

When talking with small business owners and entrepreneurs about branding, there is an inkling among them that they can "outsource" their brand to a designer they found on 99designs or an ad agency.

While you can outsource to a designer for a logo, that logo does not create a brand, nor does it have a brand strategy behind it.

Designers and ad agencies are subject-matter experts who help you visually and concisely communicate your brand message. However, having them create a logo for you, or come up with a tag line will not *"create your brand."* See *Myth 1.*

As a brand strategist, I guide entrepreneurs and organizations through the process of developing a strategy that appeals to the core values of the organization that can then be executed by their team.

Only then, once the values are set, the guiding principles are adapted, and there is a clear vision, mission, and brand promise, do we begin to conceptualize visual graphics, icons, colors, and design elements. Why? In order for the visuals and messaging to connect with their audience there must be meaning behind them.

Myth 3: Branding is a necessary expense but it doesn't provide any ROI

Not true at all.

Those who do not control their brand end up allowing harmful outside influences to take over. This is the fastest way to devalue your brand. Without a brand strategy and clear foundation, your organization will be a slab of clay for anyone else to mold however he pleases.

In small companies, you may see one or two employees who take an idea and run with it. They go against the grain of the partners or founders, knowing they have the flexibility because there isn't a set of core beliefs outlined by the organization that is clear to all employees.

What does this do to the brand long term? It creates fragmented experiences, makes clients choose individuals to work with instead of the company as a whole, and divides employees to where the culture and morale suffer. In turn, the brand suffers.

Brand strategy is as much about influence as it is about engagement and interaction with your target audience. Branding touches and influences all parts of an organization, both internally and externally. Misalignment between your marketing messaging and your internal operations hurt long-term return on investment.

We now know, thanks to neuroscience and psychology that emotions drive decision-making. Brands are a vehicle to engage their customers on an emotional level.

We now know that the deeper the relationship between a customer and brand, the greater likelihood of the customer willing to pay higher prices for products or services, which results in a higher return on investment overall for the brand.

Myth4: My business is too small to need a brand

Stop. If you are going to survive in the extremely competitive business world, you're going to have to learn to **think bigger**.

There are many opportunities for small businesses that are highly organized with a clear brand message to be ultra-successful. No matter the size of your organization, having a clear set of beliefs for your brand not only sets you apart from your competitors, it shows that your organization has a purpose, a vision and a mission on how it will achieve its goals.

People want to do business with brands they trust, no matter the size.
Your organization should be highly efficient and clear on its mission while small so that when if or when the time comes to scale up, it will be a much smoother process.

You can realize your dreams much faster when you are able to clearly communicate them and a process in place to guide you.

When organizations scale up but do not have their foundation in place, it causes growing pains that can rip the organization apart.

Gaps become amplified, broken processes are emphasized, and the entire organization suffers as they try to strap everything together in a haphazard rush-job to try and continue meeting their deadlines.

Laying the foundation helps resolve a lot of these conflicts as a company grows. In fact, the number one reason companies have growing pains is because they lack clear communication as to who they are, what they stand for, and why they exist.

Answer these questions and everything else starts to become clear.

Now that we have these limiting beliefs about branding and brand strategy out of our heads and debunked, let's get on to discussing how you can set your organization up for success.

Are you ready?

Chapter 2:

Our Approach to Brand Strategy

Define what your brand stands for, its core values and tone of voice, and then communicate consistently in those terms.
> -   *Simon Mainwaring*

Many see branding and brand strategy as structural backbone of an organization. In order to establish internal and external communication and connect with an audience, an organization must understand who it is, what it stands for, and what it values.

Without these vital pieces creating a solid structural foundation, the brand is often seen as surface-level and the customer attaches very little, if any, meaning behind the façade.

Customers are sophisticated. They can see through an organization's surface branding if there's nothing but that thin veil to present its values.

Seven-Part Framework

Through in-depth research, I have discovered seven universal truths or axioms that exist in all organizations, no matter the size or industry. The benefits of the Axioms reach into every corner of the organization, touching sales, marketing customer service, manufacturing, finance, retail, HR, IT and operations of every kind. In short, the Axioms are how some organizations deliver consistent and measurable brand experiences.

The following are the seven Axioms:
1. **Purpose** – Gives an organization clear meaning.
2. **Mission** – Provide actionable direction forward.
3. **Story** – Compelling storylines connect people.
4. **Design** – Engages in all the senses to immerse the customer.
5. **Culture** – Precise language, values, and built environments influence company culture.
6. **Metrics** – Detailed metrics can gauge the pulse a company's performance.

7. **Platform** – Engaging platforms enhance brand experiences.

Internal operational performance directly impacts brand perception and brand trust. Organizations want their audience to believe in what they have to offer.

They want to be known as a trustworthy company because those that deliver consistently keep a large and wide network of dedicated followers. The way to become a brand that delivers consistently is to have heightened internal operations that run like a well-oiled machine.

When a brand is aligned across all seven Axioms, the following is likely to occur:

- They dramatically outperform those that are not aligned.
- Optimized processes are faster, more elegant, and more efficient (both internally and client-facing).
- Teams in sync seem to self-actuate more efficient processes.

When all seven Axioms are synced, the brand performs at its best. However, when one or two of the Axioms falter or breakdown, it begins to cause friction, grinding, and fragmentation.

These internal operational performance hiccups disrupt the experience for the end user, causing the brand perception to weaken or sometimes even shatter altogether.

Each axiom plays a crucial role in the overall brand strategy and contributes to the operational performance of the organization. In this book, we'll be looking at elements from a few of the Axioms and going into detail as to how they form the foundation for an unshakable brand.

This framework and methodology guide our work with clients, as well as our own brand strategy as a company.

Brand Strategy Influences All Aspects of an Organization

Brand strategy is an underlying current that flows just below the surface of the company. It's the system that all aspects of the company adhere to in order to run in a smooth, cohesive way.

It is the organization's backbone to which all decisions stem from so that when they are made, the company knows that each decision aligns perfectly.

When a brand makes a decision that misaligns with its core values and beliefs, you can imagine it like the misalignment of your spine: balance is thrown, new aches and pains arise, and the system begins to falter unless adjusted.

Without a cohesive brand strategy, decision-making can be difficult as there might not be a clear way to gauge the decision's possible success.

It is because of this that many have turned to brand strategy to assist in this process. Brand strategy influences and amplifies core beliefs across an organization so that everyone within the company can make decisions that work within the shared strategy.

When a company chooses to go in a certain direction against some or all of its values that the brand strategy had outlined, emotions come into play from board members, customers, and employees alike. That is because the brand has strayed from its values. Think about the following aspects of your company and how brand perception affects each one:

- Business operations
- The look and feel of your retail store/office
- Employees dress code
- Customer service policies
- The look and feel of your marketing materials (website, app, social media channels)
- Pricing
- Language used in marketing messages, sales pitches, brand experiences
- Positioning in the marketplace
- Customer experience

Each of these areas mentioned is influenced by the brand strategy that is set by the organization. In order to ensure each of these elements is in alignment with the brand, a strategy must include the foundational components and *GroundWork* that were previously established.

It's through these major factors that the direction and belief system of the organization is set in motion.

In short, they are all linked. When one falters, the others break in a chain reaction.

Inside-Out Approach

My approach to brand strategy is from the inside out. All of my research and strategies involve crystal clear transparency as to who a brand is and what its values, beliefs, purpose, vision, mission, and promise to its customers are.

BrandedWorld.co invests heavily in developing a brand foundation, as it becomes the navigator that points the company in the right direction so that it can steer its brand towards a shining and successful future.

Because brand strategy influences all aspects of an organization and all pieces of communication, getting clear on who the brand is and what it believes in is critically important.

Overlooking these elements would be ineffective. For a client, picking a company to work with without knowing these elements would be similar to playing *Russian roulette.*

You want to make these elements as transparent as possible. You want them woven into your brand culture so that your clients can make a wise, informed decision when they choose you. We have already discussed how smart our audience is, so it's important that we give them every chance to make those intelligent decisions about you.

Chapter 3:

How Do You Create Meaningful Brand Experiences?

We've all experienced business interactions that we'd care not to remember. You know, that busy sandwich shop that is so rushed, it doesn't get your order right and pushes you along among the sea of other customers.

Then you get back to your desk, fully excited to dig in, only to come up with something that is vaguely similar to the actual thing you ordered. Sound familiar?

Or maybe it's the rude, overworked flight attendant who bumps into your shoulder, tells you they are out of the one meal that sounds somewhat edible, and then hands you an entertainment device with a discolored screen.

Or the team of consultants you hire to help solve a critical engineering feat, only to have them underperform throughout the process, leaving you feeling uneasy about the final product.

These are all brand experiences we deal with frequently. These experiences shape our perception of the brand, of the individuals, and quickly define how we feel about doing business with them, if ever again.

That's not to say that people who work in these companies don't have off-days, or they are dealing with their own issues and that they shouldn't be cut a bit of slack. What I'm saying is that the organization is doing a disservice to their employees, and thus their customers, by not communicating a clear set of values and beliefs.

It's the small breaks in the organization's brand that create many of these blips that cause bad experiences. There are ways to reduce or even eliminate most of these issues and they all have to do with *GroundWork.*

Meaningful Brand Experiences Start with a Set of Core Beliefs

Let's get personal for a bit. As an entrepreneur, you may have struggled to define who you are and what you stand for. Your entrepreneurial endeavors were more of an exploration of who you want to become.

And then, over time, you start to understand more and more about yourself. You begin to define your purpose in life, the work you want to do, and your incredible reason for being.

You have a mission, a purpose, and a dream that you are continuously working towards. Things suddenly begin to fall in place. You more easily make connections, grow your network, and make new friends. People begin seeking you out for advice about that passion you've worked to cultivate into a business.

You see yourself as an authority and others are beginning to validate this
What changed?

Somewhere along the way, you got clear on who you are, what your purpose is, and how you are to achieve it.

These same three revelations can be applied to your organization and the brand you are working tirelessly to develop. It doesn't just work for your own identity, but it works for your company's as well.

When you can define your company's core beliefs, they can become consistent, measurable pieces of the experience your clients will have. It's through these experiences that your customer will then be able to see what your company's beliefs are and they will be able to expect these same experiences every time.

Laying the Foundation

I speak with a lot of creative entrepreneurs. I love their energy, enthusiasm, optimism, and plans for taking over the world. I thrive off the deeply positive "let's get after it and change the world" kind of conversations. As I go deeper into understanding their passion and ideas, I begin to try and look at the foundation they are building for themselves.

Whether they realize it or not, they are forming a foundation. Some are stronger than others, but the components do not change. The five foundational components for an unshakable brand are:

- Vision
- Brand Promise

- Mission
- Core Values
- Guiding Principles

All communication, internal and external, is derived from these foundational components. If these have not been clearly thought out, applied, and adapted among the entire team, the brand will struggle to move forward while it's not united.

Imagine trying to win a three-legged race with a loosely tied rope connecting the two partners. Without that grip, the partners have to compensate and find other ways to try and sync their steps to run together.

Leaving even one of these five components out of a brand strategy will loosen the rope. You want the rope to be as tight as possible so there is little room for error.

The next chapter dives into each of these five foundational components, which is the *GroundWork* that will set a brand up for success.

We'll go into detail in each, understand what they are, why they are critical, and what best practices you can take action on today. We'll also share several examples of each, analyzing brands against the best practices to show you how you can do the same.

Let's roll up our sleeves. It's time to get into the details.

Chapter 4:

Unpacking the Foundational Elements

The Vision Statement

"A leader has the vision and conviction that a dream can be achieved. He inspires the power and energy to get it done."

- Ralph Lauren

My first experience working with and understanding vision statements came from my time consulting to the United States Air Force. The USAF is highly organized when it comes to developing strategic plans for the future.

A big portion of the work involved in strategic planning for the military is developing a Vision that the installation Commander can believe in.

Sometimes, it was about the future plans for the site, and sometimes it was more about getting consensus and buy-in from top brass in order to move a plan forward and begin the process of requesting funds from Congress.

This showed me that the importance of the vision, what the future would look like, and how it would positively impact the region we were in really mattered.

It mattered more than the engineering required, more than the electrical output necessary, and more than the thickness of the windows, doors, and walls. Those were all secondary details.

If the Commander could not understand the Vision of the overall project and get behind it to help facilitate its momentum forward, the project stalled.

The Commander has to believe that the dream, the vision, can actually be achieved. They then inspire the power, energy, and momentum to get it done.

What It Is

A Vision Statement gives definition to the dream and guidance to the organization. Organizations are created out of a need to fulfill dreams, solve problems, and improve the lives of others. The vision statement is used to provide the clarity needed to accomplish all of these lofty goals. It acts as a cornerstone for everything done within the organization that ensures that the company stays true to why it exists.

The *Walt Disney Company*'s vision statement is "*to make people happy.*" Everything that Disney produces, distributes, and provides is done so with the purpose of making people happy.

Why Is It Critical?

The Vision statement that is developed and adopted by the organization will determine the marketing, operations, and other skill-sets necessary to see it through. The goals, actions and measurement criteria are driven by the Vision.

Best Practices for Vision Statements

As one of the foundational pillars, I have researched and analyzed over fifty vision statements from both nonprofit and for-profit organizations. Analyzing both the content and length, the following have been determined as best practices for effective vision statements.

- **The Best Vision Statements are inspirational, clear, memorable, and concise.**
  Vision statements share the organization's dream with the masses. As such, they should empower employees and excite potential and existing clients. Short, memorable phrases can connect much more easily than longer, drawn out descriptions.

- **A Vision Statement should aim to be no more than 15 words maximum.**
  This guideline excludes brand references. Again, shorter is better.

- **The Vision Statement references measured goals.**
  While the Vision is a concise statement, keywords or a short phrase (1-2 words)

can act as a signal towards a goal that the organization has defined. Keywords in the statement can refer to the goal.

- **The Vision Statement identifies the organization's ideal audience.**
While staying at the broad level, the Vision should identify a segment of the population. Identifying the people you are aiming to help makes the statement more relatable. (Identifying a segment of the population may include words such as "world," if that applies to your organization.)

Exercise: Write Your Vision Statement

Analysis of Vision Statements

I've provided a detailed analysis of ten of the top brands spanning both for-profit and nonprofit organizations.

The goal is to get you thinking about your Vision statement and how it can be improved in order to have a larger impact on your ideal audience.

Look back at the vision statement you wrote in the last section. After analyzing these statements, how can you improve yours?

American Express
Vision: *the world's most respected service brand*
Word Count: 6 (15 maximum)
Measured Goal: most respected brand
Audience Identified: everyone (the world's population)

The Walt Disney Company
Vision: *to make people happy*
Word Count: 4 (15 maximum)
Measured Goal: make people happy
Audience Identified: everyone (the world's population)
Feeding America
Vision: *A hunger-free America*

Word Count: 4 (15 maximum)
Measured Goal: ridding America of hunger
Audience Identified: United States of America

Google

Vision: *To provide access to the world's information in one click*
Word Count: 10 (15 maximum)
Measured Goal: access to world's information
Audience Identified: everyone (the world's population)

Habitat for Humanity

Vision: *A world where everyone has a decent place to live*
Word Count: 10 (15 maximum)
Measured Goal: everyone has a place to live comfortably
Audience Identified: everyone (the world's population)

Hilton Worldwide

Vision: *to fill the earth with the light and warmth of hospitality*
Word Count: 11 (15 maximum)
Measured Goal: add light and warmth of hospitality to the world
Audience Identified: everyone (the world's population)

Human Rights Campaign
Vision: *Equality for everyone*
Word Count: 3 (15 maximum)
Measured Goal: equality for everyone
Audience Identified: everyone (the world's population)

The Humane Society
Vision: *To compassionately and responsibly create a more humane world for animals*
Word Count: 11 (15 maximum)
Measured Goal: equality for everyone
Audience Identified: everyone (the world's population)

Teach for America
Vision: *One day, all children in this nation will have the opportunity to attain an excellent education*
Word Count: 16 (15 maximum)
Measured Goal: all children will attain an excellent education
Audience Identified: children

Toys R Us
Vision: *to put joy in kids' hearts and a smile on parents' faces*
Word Count: 12 (15 maximum)
Measured Goal: add light and warmth of hospitality to the world

Audience Identified: everyone (the world's population)

The Brand Promise

Great companies that build an enduring brand have an emotional relationship with customers that have no barrier. And that emotional relationship is one of the most important characteristics, which is trust.
- *Howard Schultz - CEO, Starbucks*

Amazon.com has built an incredible reputation by delivering on fulfillment.

The online retail pioneer has been relentless in its pursuit to continuously expand its ability to deliver on its brand promise of *"consistently delivering an exceptional customer experience."* It has achieved this success by being reliable, anticipatory, and cost-effective.

Through its consistent efforts to deliver exceptional customer service, Amazon has established itself as an essential part of its customers' lives. What you expect is what you get.

Where brands get into trouble is when they over promise and under deliver. In the professional services arena, consultants can get into the habit of over-promising on what they will deliver, even when the budget simply will not allow it.

In an effort to please the client, the consultant rationalizes that any loss they incur on this project will be more than made up with for the next project from this same client. While the consultant may get the next project from the same client, the bar has just been raised.

From the client's perspective, the consultant over promised a set of project deliverables at a low fee. Now expectations have been set. Any new projects from the client will be expected at this higher bar.

The consultant, unbeknownst to him, just created a vicious, downward spiral due to a lack of expectation management. Worse, the brand perception may suffer due to the fact that they over promised and under delivered.

Trust could be impacted and a relationship could be broken because of this new tension. Personalized customer service enhances any brand experience, though the line must be held at the brand promise of the company. Any time an individual goes beyond the brand promise of the company the brand suffers.

The individual may get a personal win, but in the long term, it hurts the company brand. In order for the company brand to win, it must adopt and align itself with what the individual is promising. That gets tricky when a brand begins to grow. How can the company stay consistent if multiple individuals are going in all different directions? It simply isn't sustainable.

What It Is

The Brand Promise is a strategic tool to hold the organization accountable for delivering a consistent brand experience to its clients. As a foundational element, it is what helps to create an authentic brand.

The promise outlines the objective of the company and explains what the customer can expect to receive or experience from the organization.

The Brand Promise is only as effective as it is measurable and meaningful. Let's define each of these areas further.

Measurable

The Brand promise needs to be a measurable one that has calculated delivery that the ideal audience can expect.

BMW's brand promise is *"the ultimate driving machine."* Throughout every interaction, touch point, and engagement with BMW, the customer is being promised that if they were to purchase, they would be getting the most efficient and elegant vehicle, resulting in the *ultimate driving machine.*

Internally, *BMW* most likely has a measurable definition of the phrase *"ultimate driving machine."* This definition that is unique to BMW is used to break down the promise and calculate its success. Criteria to measure may include data from the closest competitors and customer satisfaction surveys.

Meaningful

The Brand Promise is not a piece of marketing fluff. When an organization makes a promise to its clients, the clients expect it to be kept. This is the essence of the Brand Promise.

It's easier to see if brands are keeping their promises in companies that offer tangible products. For example, if a restaurant's brand promise is to offer high-quality food at fast-casual prices, a $40 hamburger would not be accepted. No one would pay it.

Within the professional services industry, keeping the Brand Promise and making individual promises tends to confuse and frustrate the client and the organization. Imagine an organization that offers planning services for conventions. If the organization's Brand Promise is to deliver quality conferences to clients, all individuals should work towards this goal.

When individuals are put in charge of keeping this promise to a client and the promise is not clearly stated, an individual might slip and make a promise that was never intended for the business to make.

Let's say, for example, an employee of the convention planning company promises to do some accounting work for the client's taxes on top of booking speakers for the upcoming convention.

They are breaking the Brand Promise, as there was never anything mentioned on accounting. No longer are they working together on a measurable goal, but they are going into a realm that is not measured or promised. If the outcome of the accounting venture proves to be a huge failure, the client is going to blame the organization. The organization will have to explain that they don't even do taxes to begin with.

This gap causes friction, shatters the brand experience, and creates an inconsistent pattern of deliverables. By having a clear brand promise, employees and team members can get behind it, focusing on delivering consistent results to their clients.

Why Is It Critical?

When a brand consistently communicates that it will provide x, y, and z and then delivers x, y, and z, it is building brand value. Brand value is a form of trust that the consumer or client has for the organization. The client believes in what the organization stands for, the services or products they deliver, and how they deliver them.

Having a measurable and meaningful brand promise as a strategic tool gives your organization an advantage in two ways. First, it communicates clearly to your ideal audience what you promise to deliver. This creates transparency and builds trust. And second, it gives your organization a tool to measure your performance with. You can quickly understand how the company is performing based on the percentage of promises delivered. (Total customers divided by missed promises equals brand promise percentage.)

This quick tool can give you insight into where the brand needs to improve their process in order to deliver an exceptional expcrience.

Best Practices for Brand Promises

Brand Promises should be clear, concise, and measurable. Similar to Vision and Mission statements, the Brand Promise should be used as a tool to quickly assess if the product or service has met the brand promise.

Strong brand promises have the following characteristics:

- Simple
- Realistic
- Indicative
- Actionable

Analyzing both content and length, the following have been determined as best practices for effective brand promises.

- **The Best Brand Promises are simple, realistic, indicative, and actionable.**

- **A Brand Promise should be no more than 10 words if possible.**
  While the average of the brand promises analyzed was approximately six words, keep in mind that the promise should be simple, realistic, indicative, and actionable.

That is a lot of information to put in so few words.

• **The Brand Promise is Measurable.** Like the Vision Statement, choose one or two keywords in the promise statement that can be tied back to a measurable objective. This will provide the organization a litmus test in which the team can quickly assess their performance based on the statement and choose how to move forward accordingly.

• **The Brand Promise is Meaningful.** Choose your words carefully and ensure that each has meaning that drives home the message of the organization. The statement is a promise that the organization must believe in and work tirelessly to deliver on consistently.

Exercise: Write Your Brand Promise

Analysis of Brand Promises

The following collections of brand promises are from nonprofit and for-profit organizations. The goal is to get you thinking about your brand promise and how it can be improved upon in order to hold your organization accountable. It will be used to help deliver consistently on the promise stated.

Of the organizations analyzed, the average word count of the brand promise was approximately 6.3 words. The examples below show a range of length and styles of brand promises, yet all provide a clear, concise, and memorable statement.

BMW

Brand Promise: *The ultimate driving machine*

Word Count: 5 (10 words maximum)

Meaningful: The phrase implies high quality, superb craftsmanship, and excellent handling.

Measurable: The phrase 'Ultimate Driving Machine' can be tied back to the performance of the product (all lines and models) and how customers perceive the product.

Walt Disney's Disneyland

Brand Promise: *The happiest place on Earth*

Word Count: 5 (10 words maximum)

Meaningful: The phrase is simple, indicative, and realistic. Everything Disney produces and distributes is meant to make people happy.

Measurable: The phrase can be measured based on customer's feedback as to whether they love the experiences available throughout the *Disneyland* theme park.

Marriott

Brand Promise: *Quiet luxury. Crafted experiences. Intuitive service.*

Word Count: 6 (10 words maximum)
Meaningful: The phrase is simple, indicative, actionable and realistic. The phrase quickly explains the experience you will have when staying at their hotel.

Measurable: The phrase can be measured in three parts.

'*Quiet luxury*' indicates a soothing, relaxing atmosphere. If a guest complains of loud music or disturbances staff know that the hotel is not meeting its promise to its guests.

'*Crafted Experience*' indicates that the guest will be taken care of in a highly detailed way. If a guest does not enjoy their stay that implies that the experience was not executed to the hotels' best ability.

'*Intuitive Service*' indicates that the hotel will anticipate the needs of their guests before the guest requests them. If a guest requests something that was not first anticipated, that is an indication that the hotel is not holding up their promise.

Starbucks

Brand Promise: *Our promise: love it or let us know*

Word Count: 8 (10 words maximum)

Meaningful: The phrase is simple, indicative, and realistic. If you are not satisfied with your handcrafted drink, let a barista know and they will make it right.

Measurable: The phrase can be measured based on customer's feedback as to whether they love their drink or are letting baristas know.

The Virgin Group

Brand Promise: *To be genuine, fun, contemporary, and different in everything we do at a reasonable price.*

Word Count: 15 (10 words maximum)

Meaningful: The phrase quickly describes the experience you will have with any of Virgin's brands.

Measurable: The phrase has four keywords that describe the values of the brand. Each can be measured based on the individual customer experience for each of Virgin's over 400 companies.

'*Genuine*' indicates an authentic brand that is honest and has the highest integrity.

'*Fun*' indicates experiences and products will be light-hearted, safe, and enjoyable.
'*Contemporary*' indicates that the brand is up to date with the latest trends and technology to provide the best customer experience possible.

'*Different*' indicates that the brand has defined themselves apart from competitors and will offer the customer a unique experience.

Each of these keywords can be used as a checklist to make sure that the customer is satisfied with their product, service, or experience from *The Virgin Group*.

The Mission Statement

A mission statement is not something you write overnight... But fundamentally, your mission statement becomes your constitution, the solid expression of your vision and values. It becomes the criterion by which you measure everything else in your life.

- Stephen Covey

What It Is

Mission statements are usually the most visual element. It's the one you've most likely heard about most often. Your company's mission statement is your opportunity to define the company's goals, ethics, culture, and norms for decision-making.

The best mission statements define a company's goals in at least three dimensions: what the company does for its customers, what it does for its employees, and what it does for its owners. Some of the best mission statements also extend themselves to include fourth and fifth dimensions: what the company does for its community, and for the world.

Why Is It Critical?

Well-defined and succinct mission statements provide clear direction to all employees and executives. Ideally, all team members would be able to recite the mission statement by heart, as it is embedded into the cultural fabric of the brand.

Further, each team member should have a clear understanding of their role and how what they do plays a bigger part in achieving the mission for the brand. This deeper understanding allows team members to take more ownership over their position within the company, therefore working towards a common goal.

The *United States Air Force* has one of the clearest and simplest mission statements. Throughout my years as a strategic planner and consultant to the Air Force, I was always impressed that no matter whom I spoke with, no matter their rank or position, they knew not only the Air Force's mission but their department's mission as well.

They were able to clearly and succinctly state how their department's mission contributed to achieving the larger mission.

The Air Force's Mission is, *"To Fly, Fight, and Win...in Air, Space and Cyberspace."*

This incredible knowledge and attention to detail from a strategic perspective gives the Air Force an advantage as Airmen are proactively engaged and committed to serving.

Taking these same attributes and applying them to the civilian world is rather difficult. Brands that have developed the *GroundWork* and actively weave them into the fabric of the culture stand a better chance of developing a team that takes real pride in helping the organization further its mission.

Best Practices for Mission Statements

As one of the foundational pillars, I have researched and analyzed over fifty mission statements across a variety of organizations, sizes, and industries. Analyzing both content and length, the following have been determined as best practices for effective mission statements.

- **Aim for approximately 20 words max.** This is a rule of thumb. With the idea that your team can recite it word for word, shorter is best.

- **Include keywords (three, max) that describe the organization's products or services.** What are the keywords used to describe your brand? Using one or two of these in your Mission helps to create a stronger, cohesive brand.

- **Use action-oriented words (active voice)** Active voice denotes action. Action-oriented words describe the present and create an exciting statement.
- **Does the Mission define what the company does for its customers?**

The Mission should succinctly state what the company does for its customers. The Air Force flies, fights, and wins in the areas of air, space, and cyberspace. From a customer perspective (US citizen), you can quickly understand how the Air Force offers protection.

- **Does the Mission define what the company does for its employees?**

The Mission should succinctly state what the company does for its employees. As US Airmen, they understand what the Air Force does (fly, fight, and win) and in where (air, space, and cyberspace). US Airman, with specific skill sets, can fit into one of the broad areas that are described in the Mission.

- **Does the Mission define what the company does for its owners?**

The Mission should succinctly state what the company does for its owners. Using the Air Force as an example, the Government could be considered the owners.

The Government can quickly assess what the Air Force does (fly, fight, and win) and in what capacity and what areas (air, space, cyberspace), which allows them to better integrate with the other military services like the Navy, Marines, and Army.

Exercise: Write Your Mission Statement

Analysis of Mission Statements

Some of the best Missions out of my research included both nonprofit and for-profit organizations. This section will highlight the top ten Mission statements, analyzing each against the guidelines above.

The goal is to get you thinking about your Mission and how it can be improved upon in order to have a larger impact on your ideal audience.

Chevron

Mission Statement: *To be the global energy company most admired for its people, partnership and performance*

Word Count: 14 (20 words maximum)
Keywords: global, energy, people, partnerships, and performance

Active Voice: Yes

For Customers: Customers can quickly assess *Chevron*'s dedication to its people, partnerships, and performance as a global energy company.

For Employees: Employees of *Chevron* understand what the company is striving for and what the company emphasizes (*most admired for its people, partnerships, and performance*).

For Owners: The owners/shareholders of *Chevron* can quickly assess the performance by posing the three phrases as questions. They can ask three questions to get a quick assessment:

- Is *Chevron* most admired for its people?
- Is *Chevron* most admired for its partnerships?
- Is *Chevron* most admired for its performance?

Facebook

Mission Statement: *To give people the power to share and make the world more open and connected*

Word Count: 15 (20 words maximum)
Keywords: people, share, world, connected, power.

Active Voice: Yes

For Customers: Users of *Facebook* can quickly assess and relate to the mission of giving people the power to share and connect with others around the world.

For Employees: Employees of *Facebook* understand the mission is to give their users the power to share and become connected with others around the world.

For Owners: The owners/shareholders of *Facebook* can quickly assess the performance by posing two of the phrases as questions. They can ask two questions to get a quick assessment:

- Is *Facebook* providing enough opportunities and power for its users to share?
- Is *Facebook* making the world more open and connected through its products, services, and initiatives?

Ford

Mission Statement: *We go further to make our cars better, our employees happier, and our planet a better place to be.*

Word Count: 19 (20 words maximum)

Keywords: cars better, employees, happier, planet

Active Voice: Yes

For Customers: Customers can easily relate to *Ford*'s mission of going the extra mile to make their cars better (*We go further to make our cars better*).

For Employees: Employees of *Ford* understand that *Ford* has three main objectives: to make better cars, employees happy, and the planet a better place to be. From the employee perspective, *Ford*'s mission clearly states that happiness among their employees is central to achieving success.

For Owners: The owners/shareholders of *Ford* can quickly assess the performance by posing three of the phrases as questions. They can ask three questions to get a quick assessment:

- Is *Ford* going far enough to make their cars better?
- Is *Ford* going far enough to make their employees happy?
- Is *Ford* going far enough to make the planet better (cleaner, safer, etc.)?

The New York Public Library

Mission Statement: *To inspire lifelong learning, advance knowledge, and strengthen our communities*

Word Count: 10 (20 words maximum)

Keywords: learning, knowledge, communities

Active Voice: Yes

For Customers: Customers can quickly understand what *The New York Public Library* stands for (*inspire lifelong learning, advance knowledge*) and what it is working to achieve (*strengthen our communities*).

For Employees: Employees of *The New York Public Library* understand what the library stands for, what it is working towards, and how they fit into the equation (*inspiring and advocating for lifelong learning, advance knowledge, and strengthening the community.*)

For Owners: The owners of *The New York Public Library* can quickly assess the performance by using each phrase as a separate goal. They can ask three questions to get a quick assessment:

- How is *The New York Public Library* inspiring lifelong learning?
- How is *the New York Public Library* inspiring advance knowledge?
- How is *The New York Public Library* strengthening our communities?

Nordstrom

Mission Statement: *Offer the customer the best possible service, selection, quality and value*

Word Count: 11 (20 words maximum)
Keywords: customer, best service, best selection, best quality, best value
Active Voice: Yes

For Customers: Customers can quickly assess that *Nordstrom*'s has their best interest by offering the best possible service, selection, quality, and value.

For Employees: Employees of *Nordstrom*'s understand that the customer is the main objective. Employees are to ensure that the customer receives the best possible service, selection, quality, and value.

For Owners: The owners/shareholders of *Nordstrom* can quickly assess the performance by posing four of the phrases as questions. They can ask four questions to get a quick assessment:

- Is *Nordstrom* providing the best possible customer service?

- Is *Nordstrom* providing the best possible selection?
- Is *Nordstrom* providing the best possible quality?
- Is *Nordstrom* providing the best possible value?

Oxfam

Mission Statement: *To create lasting solutions to poverty, hunger, and social injustice*

Word Count: 10 (20 words maximum)

Keywords: poverty, hunger, social injustice

Active Voice: Yes

For Customers: Customers can quickly understand *Oxfam*'s mission and what they are working to achieve (*create lasting solutions to poverty, hunger, and social injustice*).

For Employees: Employees of *Oxfam* clearly understand that the mission is to create lasting solutions for poverty, hunger and social injustice.

For Owners: The owners of *Oxfam* can quickly assess the performance by using each phrase as a separate goal. They can ask three questions to get a quick assessment:

- How is *Oxfam* creating lasting solutions to poverty?
- How is *Oxfam* creating lasting solutions to hunger?
- How is *Oxfam* creating lasting solutions to social injustice?

Starbucks

Mission Statement: *To inspire and nurture the human spirit- one person, one cup, and one neighborhood at a time*

Word Count: 17 (20 words maximum)

Keywords: inspire, nurture, human spirit, neighborhood

Active Voice: Yes

For Customers: Customers can quickly assess and relate to *Starbucks*' mission of inspiring and nurturing the human spirit – one person, one cup, and one neighborhood at a time.

For Employees: Employees of *Starbucks* understand the mission of *Starbucks* is to inspire and nurture the human spirit through the hand crafted drinks they make.

For Owners: The owners/shareholders of *Starbucks* can quickly assess the performance by posing two of the phrases as questions. They can ask two questions to get a quick assessment:

- Is *Starbucks* inspiring and nurturing each customer that comes through their doors?
- Is *Starbucks* inspiring the neighborhoods where they are located?

TED

Mission Statement: *Spreading Ideas*

Word Count: 2 (20 words maximum)

Keywords: Ideas

Active Voice: Yes

For Customers: Customers can quickly understand *TED*'s model of distributing ideas

For Employees: Employees of *TED* clearly understand that the mission of *TED* is to spread ideas globally.

For Owners: The owners of *TED* can quickly assess how the business model is performing by understanding how *TED* videos and content are being distributed and where new opportunities for distribution may be.

The Humane Society

Mission Statement: *Celebrating animals, confronting cruelty*

Word Count: 4 (20 words maximum)

Keywords: animals, cruelty

Active Voice: Yes

For Customers: Customers can quickly understand what *The Humane Society* is focused on (*celebrating animals and confronting cruelty*).

For Employees: Employees of The *Humane Society* have a clear picture of the organization's mission: celebrate animals and confront cruelty of animals.

For Owners: The owners of *The Humane Society* can quickly assess the performance by posing the two phrases as questions. They can ask two questions to get a quick assessment:

- How does *The Humane Society* celebrate animals?
- How does *The Humane Society* confront cruelty towards animals?

USO

Mission Statement: *Lifts the spirits of America's troops and their families*

Word Count: 9 (20 words maximum)

Keywords: America's troops, families, lift spirits

Active Voice: Yes

For Customers: Customers can quickly understand *USO*'s mission and who it is for (*lift the spirits of America's troops and their families).*

For Employees: Employees of *USO* clearly understand the mission is to lift the spirits of America's troops and their families (This is accomplished through their programs and live events held around the world at US military installations).

For Owners: The owners of *USO* can quickly assess the performance by using the phrase as a question. They can ask a simple question to get a quick assessment:

- How is the *USO* lifting the spirits of America's troops and their families?

Virgin Atlantic

Mission Statement: *To embrace the human spirit and let it fly.*

Word Count: 9 (20 words maximum)

Keywords: human spirit, fly

Active Voice: Yes

For Customers: Customers can quickly assess *Virgin Atlantic's* mission of embracing the human spirit and letting it fly.

For Employees: Employees of *Virgin Atlantic* understand that the company values the human spirit and providing a fun customer experience.

For Owners: The owners and shareholders of *Virgin Atlantic* can quickly assess the performance by posing the two phrases as questions. They can ask two questions to get a quick assessment:

- Is *Virgin Atlantic* embracing the human spirit in all that they do?
- Is *Virgin Atlantic* letting it fly?

Core Values

Brands are facing a new competitive landscape in which self-definition; core values and purpose will increasingly define their ability to reach customers that only allow what is meaningful in their lives to pass through their filter.

- *Simon Mainwaring*

To really understand your ideal audience, you must know who they are not just as much as you know on a deeper level. Core values are a way to reach ideal customers while filtering out those that don't fit. It is OK to not be a fit for everyone. If your brand is trying to appeal to everyone, you end up appealing to no one.

What It Is

The core values are the characteristics the company believes it exhibits and perpetuates. With every interaction with the company, they believe that they are acting with their core values that could include characteristics like trust, honor, bravery, and creativity.

When you think of core values, you might think of marketing fluff. You may even think of core values as nothing more than a list of buzzwords that sound good and fill corporate brochures and websites.

However, c*ore values* are the deeply ingrained principles that guide all of a company's actions; they serve as its cultural cornerstones. When you take pride in the values that the organization stands for, it gives them a much deeper meaning.

Another myth is that for core values to be effective, there must be a consensus among all team members. In fact, values initiatives have nothing to do with building consensus.

They are about imposing a set of fundamental, strategically sound beliefs on a broad group of people. They begin to define the culture, and therefore how people will fit into the organization.

"It's not hard to make decisions when you know what your values are."
                                              - Roy Disney

When determining a set of values, it is recommended to work in a small team. The team may include the CEO, any founders, and a handful of key employees. The objective of the core values is to lay the initial foundation that will ultimately shape the company culture.

Why Is It Critical?

Aggressively adhering to one's values can help an organization make strategic decisions. Values can be used as a strategic compass to make large decisions. Core values are a true reflection of what the company believes – and management and employees are willing to live by them.

For values to take hold in your organization, they must be woven into every process, system, product, and service offered.

This includes every employee-related process – hiring methods, performance management systems, promotions, and rewards criteria. It even applies to dismissal policies. Employees should be constantly reminded that core values form the basis for every decision the company makes.

Reinforcing values with action instills them into the culture. When employees perform at a high level, such as providing excellent customer service, the company may offer rewards such as cash and other forms of public recognition.

This produces engaged employees and that translates into hard numbers showing a positive impact for the company overall.

In a *Gallup* study[1], business units that ranked in the top 25% of their organizations for employee engagement showed:

- 22% higher profitability
- 21% higher productivity
- 10% higher customer satisfaction
- 37% lower absenteeism
- 48% fewer safety incidents

---

[1] Source: http://www.gallup.com/services/178514/state-american-workplace.aspx

- 41% fewer quality incidents (defects)

A workforce is an engine that will lead your company to growth and profitability. Employees that engage and believe in the brand and what the organization stands for having the potential to be your biggest brand ambassadors.

They positively reflect the brand to their network and in their community. The Core Values are the keystone that will give them their purpose.

Tom Peters, business guru explains what makes employee engagement so important:

"Employees' behavior has a direct impact on the bottom line, costs, revenue streams, level of productivity, customer satisfaction, even the brand- every aspect of the business is affected. If strategy and culture are not aligned, the culture may support behaviors that conflict with what has to get done- and actually, block execution of the strategy."

A recent survey published by Deloitte polled millennials on their loyalty to their companies.

The results showed that, in general, millennials express little loyalty to their current employers and many are planning near-term exits. This "*loyalty challenge*" is driven by a number of factors.

Many feel they are not being developed for leadership roles, though millennials have softened negative perceptions of corporate motivation and ethics. Millennials also cite a strong desire for alignment of values.

However, they feel that most businesses have no ambition beyond profit and there are distinct differences in what they believe the purpose of business should be and what they perceive it to currently be.

From the report, "*Millennials often put their personal values ahead of organizational goals, and several have shunned assignment (and potential employers) that conflict with their beliefs.*" [2]

These findings are drawn from Deloitte's fifth global Millennial Survey, which in 2016, focused on millennials' values and ambitions,

---

[2] Source:
http://www2.deloitte.com/global/en/pages/about-deloitte/articles/gx-millennials-shifting-business-purpose.html#values

drivers of job satisfaction, and their increasing representation on senior management teams.

Are you starting to get a sense of why core values are so powerful? Think about your brand's current core values – do they align with the best practices on the next couple pages? If so, *great*! If not, it may be time to revisit them in order to give your brand deeper meaning.

Best Practices for Core Values

- **Values should be a true reflection of what the organization believes – and what the employees are willing to live by.**

  When it comes to values, they should be true to the organization and the people that make up the organization. If everyone isn't willing to live by the values set, either those individuals need to leave, or they should reevaluate what they've created.

- **Aim for 4-10 Core Values**

  It is not necessary to have a long list of values, but rather a list of values with real meaning. If you can get the values across with four, do it. If you need a bit more, add them. The values should be something that is repeated and woven into the fabric of the culture. Therefore, keeping the list shorter can make it easier to include.

- **Core Values should be a single word or short phrase. (Less than 10 words).**

Study the examples provided. Most core values are a single word or a short phrase of fewer than ten words. Short, succinct and actionable words make them stick to the minds of your team members.

- **Choose Values related to positive characteristics of team members. This will in turn help to shape the culture**.
  This is an important guideline. By choosing values related to the positive characteristics of ideal team members, they begin to act as a filter during the hiring process.

  Embracing and living by your core values can help you find others with similar personal values that easily embrace those of the organization. Choosing values that relate to positive characteristics can filter and identify ideal team members.

Exercise: Write Your Core Values

Analysis of Core Values

Core Values come in all different forms. Some organizations have a list of values while others create a statement. The format of the values doesn't necessarily matter – it is the content and the ability to identify the core values. The below examples use a variety of different formats.

These were chosen for the purpose of showing that the guidelines above work no matter the format of the Core Values.

L.L. Bean

Core Values: Sell good merchandise at a reasonable profit, treat your customers like human beings, and they will always come back for more.

Core Values Count: 3; *L.L. Bean* embraces a statement, which all team members live by. Within the statement, there are three values that stand out:

Single or Short Phrases: The statement provides guidance on what the organization values (*good merchandise at a reasonable* *profit*), how customers should be treated (*like human beings*), and why (*they will always come back for more*).

Positive Characteristics: The statement overall has a positive tone to it, sharing how *L.L. Bean* treats its customers and how team members should act.

While the statement is less clear than a short list of values, it can still be used to gauge how an employee or team is performing. It also can be used as a filter or qualifier during the hiring process. Certain questions could be asked that relate back to the meaning of the statement.

Walmart

Core Values: excellence, customer service, and respect to employees.

Core Values Count: 3 (4 to 10)

Single or Short Phrases: Each of the three core values is either a single word (*E.g.,* excellence) or no more than a three-word phrase (*respect to employees*). These are easy to remember and embrace as part of the culture.

Positive Characteristics: The values of *Walmart* share positive characteristics of associates that work for the organization. A commitment to excellence, customer service, and respect are important characteristics that *Walmart* looks for in the individuals they hire. Using the core values helps to shape the culture of *Walmart*.

Wegman's

Core Values: "Who We Are" Values: caring, high standards, making a difference, respect, and empowerment.

Core Values Count: 5 (4 to 10)

Single or Short Phrases: 3 of the values are single words, while 2 of the values are short phrases of two and three words, respectively.

Positive Characteristics: All of the values demonstrate positive characteristics that would be ideal within individual team members. Each of the values can act as a litmus test against an individual's performance, or a team's performance as a whole.

Guiding Principles

When we began Starbucks, what I wanted to try to do was to create a set of values, guiding principles, and culture.
- Howard Schultz

Guiding principles sound daunting at first glance, but once you unpack them, they are simply statements to help keep the brand on track and moving forward. Guiding principles provide a framework for the brand, leaving enough breathing space to try new things, expand into different areas and stay within the guidelines.

What It Is

Guiding principles reflect your vision, mission, and strategic interests, core values, and the firm's core competencies. They help your organization stay on course, make decisions better and faster and allow you to keep going.

If you have a set of guiding principles, any proposed a new course of action – be it a company initiative, the introduction of a new product, or a new direction that you're about to launch off to, you would need to answer only one question:

Does it fit our firm's guiding principles?

What's more, guiding principles give additional depth to the organization. If the founders left or were gone for extended periods of time, the executives and board of directors can continue to make decisions based on the guiding principles, core values, vision, and mission without fear of harming the brand.

Why Is It Critical?

Guiding principles are the law that serves as a basis for reasoning and action, a personal code of conduct that leads, otherwise directing the movements of your organization. Guiding principles are a broad philosophy that guides the organization throughout its life in all circumstances, irrespective of changes in its goals, strategies, work type, or top management. Without them, an organization is liable to start shifting in any direction the leadership chooses.

Having a set of guiding principles for decision-making has value and makes the organization faster only if they are lived by members of the organization and enforced.

Guiding Principles Best Practices

- **The principles, as a set, form the broad philosophy that guides the organization.**
  Taking the time to write down the principles that will guide the organization allows all team members and executives to understand where the company is headed.

  The broad philosophy of the organization has now been transferred from the entrepreneur's imagination and has been documented for everyone to understand and be guided by. This provides much-needed depth to the organization, allowing executives and team members to be empowered to work towards the desired outcome.

- **The principles help you answer the question, *"does it fit our firm's guiding principles?"***
  The foundational pillars provide the organization a starting point when evaluating new business lines, acquisitions, new hires, or products/services. Make sure that the principles provide enough detail to help answer the question.

- **Guiding Principles can take several different forms; should aim to have 4-6; no more than 10 total.**
Similar to core values, guiding principles can take many different forms. For best practices, try to limit the amount of guiding principles to a maximum of ten.

Any more than that and it becomes a much more difficult task to use them as an evaluation tool. Combined with the other four pillars, it can be a lengthy, but necessary process to go through if all foundational components are evaluating new opportunities for the organization.

- **Each Principle should stand on its own and fit within the larger set. Eliminate filler words and principles that could be combined with others.**
Just as with the other pillars, the guiding principles should be actionable and measurable.
This helps the organization to use them as a tool when evaluating opportunities. Eliminate filler words and focus on how each statement can be used as an

individual tool as well as a part of the set of principles.

- **Aim to keep each Principle to no more than 10 words. (Fewer than 5 words is Best).**
Less is more. Short, actionable phrases that connect with the core values, vision, mission, and brand promise help to tie all of the foundation elements together. Guiding principles cover the broad philosophy of why the organization exists and what it provides.

Exercise: Write Your Guiding Principles

Analysis of Guiding Principles

ITW Global Automotive

ITW Global Automotive is a global industrial company that develops engineered products and specialty systems that are created and later improved in direct partnership with the company's customers.

ITW leaders apply the → *80/20 Process* to everything they do in order to get a lot of things right.

ITW Guiding Principles

We believe the future of good business is deeply rooted in the past. By following our guiding principles designed to enhance customer focus, productivity, innovation and profitability, we are able to make continual process and product improvements for customers, while producing solid results for our shareholders.

Our ability to produce commercial innovations on a continual basis for our customers is the foundation of our success.

Our main guiding principles[3] include the following:

- Decentralization: placing the businesses close to the people who buy company's products.

- *80/20 Process*: focusing on the most profitable products and customers.

Innovation: developing commercial innovations.

GP Word Count: The shortest GP is 4 words; the longest is 12. (10 words max.)

GP Count: ITW has 3 main guiding principles. (Aim between 4 and 6; max. 10)

GP's Stand Alone: Each of *ITW*'s GP's are tied to clear, measurable objectives. Each can be used as a measure of the organization individually, as well as a set of principles.
Answers the Question: Using the set of GP's, *ITW* is able to answer the question, "*does it fit*

---

[3] Source:
http://www.1000ventures.com/business_guide/im_guiding
_principles_itw.html

our guiding principles?" in terms of new initiatives, business lines, products, or services.

Facebook

Facebook's 10 Guiding Principles[4]
1. Create a Better World
2. Build a Good Team
3. Cultivate Fearlessness
4. Take Risks
5. Excite and Amaze Users
6. Commit to Simplicity
7. Move Fast and Break Things
8. Don't Let a Competitor Get Ahead of You
9. Adhere to the Process
10. Create an Exciting Workplace

GP Word Count: The shortest GP is 2 words; the longest is 8 (10 words max).

GP Count: *Facebook* has a set of 10 guiding principles (Aim between 4 and 6; max 10).

---

[4] Source:
http://www.1000ventures.com/business_guide/cs_internet _biz_facebook_10lessons.html

GP's Stand Alone: Each of *Facebook*'s GP's are simple in nature. Each can stand on its' own and makes sense. Combined, the set of GP's provide a broad philosophy of what *Facebook* is setting out to accomplish.

Answers the Question: Using the set of GP's, *Facebook* is able to answer the question, "*does it fit our guiding principles?*" in terms of new initiatives, business lines, products, or services.

Chapter 5:

Applying the Foundational Components to Brand Experiences

"Design is a plan for arranging elements in such a way as best to accomplish a particular purpose."

- Charles Eames

We now have a clear understanding of the foundational components needed to develop an unshakable brand. These components, when used within an organization, will heavily influence and guide the brand in every decision it makes.

I want to take it a step further and share two case studies of unshakable brands. We'll walk through the foundational elements of each organization and gain an understanding of what they stand for, what they value, and what they believe in.

We'll then look at how each brand brings those foundational components to life through their unique brand experiences.

Two Types of Experience Design

There are two types of experience design: *physical* and *digital*. The objective of both of these is to guide the customer through an immersive experience, influencing them along the way through visual cues, lighting, design elements, and sensory details.

Physical design leads the customer through an environment. Examples of this could be a theme park, retail store, corporate office, or open mall. In all of these examples, the design is tailored to the five senses, immersing the customer into the physical world of the brand.

Digital design leads the user through a series of pages on a website or mobile application. These platforms use different design elements and cues to focus the attention of the user towards taking an action, such as clicking on a button to download, subscribe, or join.

As experiences come to the forefront, a new hybrid experience design model is emerging. Using both physical and digital design, experiences will start to bloom between the two, creating a new type of information-infused experience.

The following case studies are two of the top brands delivering exceptional brand experiences on a consistent basis across the globe.

Case Study: *Disney*

The *Walt Disney Company* is an iconic American brand that spans the globe. *Disney* has been one of my biggest influences growing up through interacting with their movies, theme parks, and toys.

Understanding Walt Disney, Himself

Walt Disney was an American entrepreneur, animator, voice actor, and film producer. In private, he was known as being shy and insecure, but later he was known for adopting a warm and outgoing public persona.

Through this public persona, we get a look into his unobstructed imagination for creating and designing experiences that are full of magic, wonder, and dreams.

Walt's vision of a clean and safe park, fun for both adults and children, guided the company through the two-year development process when creating the *Disneyland* theme park in 1955.

Understanding The Walt Disney Company, the Brand

Many of the positive, entrepreneurial, and imaginative qualities have been adopted and integrated into the *Walt Disney Company*'s brand. Looking at the core values and guiding principles, it is absolutely clear that the brand is focused on knowing its values and explaining why exceeding customer expectations is crucial to the company's success. Through business design, the brand created their values to enhance the customer's experiences.

These principles articulate the type of culture that the *Disney* brand continues to shape and foster as it moves into the future.

The Walt Disney Company's Foundational Elements

Let's dive deep into *Disney* and understand their brand foundation. We'll then do an analysis of the foundational statements to understand what words best associate with *Disney*. This will help us understand how *Disney* brings its core beliefs to life through stores, theme parks, cruise ships, television channels, movies, and other experiences.

Vision
To make people happy – Disney Archives 2012

Mission
The Walt Disney Company's objective is to be one of the world's leading producers and providers of entertainment and information, using its portfolio of brands to differentiate its content, services and consumer products. – September 2013

Brand Promise
Where Dreams Come True

Core Values
Innovation, Quality, Community, Storytelling, Optimism, Decency

Guiding Principles[5]

1. *Know what you value and why*
2. *Demonstrate the courage of leadership*
3. *Strive for perfection and don't compromise quality.*
4. *Money is a means, not an end*
5. *Exceed customer expectations*
6. *Create valued experiences through business design*
7. *Minds create value so treat them with respect*
8. *Let creativity work for you*
9. *Think deeply from all directions*

---

[5] Source: http://www.tspg-consulting.com/printpages/9wedprinciples.pdf

Foundational Elements Analysis

Reading through *Disney*'s brand foundational components, you can quickly get a sense of what the company stands for, what the brand values within its team, and what guiding principles it establishes that moves it forward.

Founder's Words

Studying Walt Disney himself, you get a sense of who he is and what his vision for The *Walt Disney Company* was and still is today. When you hear Disney speak, he associates with words such as "wonderment", "imagination", "dreams", and "magic". These characteristics are evident in every piece of content *Disney* produces and deliver on.

Key Words

Further analyzing the brand foundation components, you can get a sense of the key words that the *Disney* brand itself wants to be known for.

Here is a short list:

- Happy
- People
- Imagination
- Wonder
- Magic
- Dreams
- Entertainment
- World
- Leader

These words are not only associative to the *Disney* brand, but they are used in the messaging to guide the user, visitor, moviegoer and step into their world.

Unpacking the Disney Experience

So much can be written and studied on how *Disney* delivers its experiences. We'll unpack a tiny percentage of one of *Disney*'s experiences: Main Street USA at *Disneyland* in Anaheim, California. We'll also look at *Disney*'s use of a mobile app and how using technology can enhance the already incredible experience the park offers.

Physical Design Experience

Looking at *Disneyland's* Main Street, USA as an example of a physical design experience, you can quickly begin to feel immersed into the imaginative and magical world of *Disney.*
Standing in the middle of Main Street facing Cinderella's castle, it appears as though the buildings lining the streets are much taller than they actually are. The use of foreshortening is a trick used in illustrations to make objects appear larger than they really are.

You'll notice the top two floors of the buildings are less than the standard height required for people to occupy them. This is done to impress upon the visitor that the Main Street is larger than life, creatively playing with the user's imagination.

Cinderella's castle also uses foreshortening to sell the illusion of being larger than life and far off in the distance, similar to the perspectives you'd see in one of *Disney*'s films. The visitor, in a state of suspended belief, has entered into the magical world of *Disney*, and while immersed in that world, they believe in the magic, building a stronger bond with the brand.

Figure 1: Sketch of Main Street USA at Disneyland, looking towards Cinderella's castle. This perspective shows the foreshortening used on the buildings to create the illusion that they are larger than they appear.

Digital Design Experience

Disney has always experimented and adopted early technology in order to enhance the experiences they create for their park visitors. The *Disneyland* app is a prime example of this. The app allows a visitor to access a virtual map of *Disneyland* in order to locate *Disney* characters, shows, events, and restaurants throughout the park. The app even allows a user to register for an attraction ahead of time to cut down on the lines.

The physical experience is enhanced by giving the visitor additional information they can access on demand through *Disney*'s app.

The visitor is then free to find the characters and when they are available, book a time slot for particular attractions, and make reservations at restaurants, thus creating a more personalized, efficient, and seamless experience.

In both the physical and digital design experiences, *Disney* has stayed true to its brand foundational components, delivering experiences that align with its core values (*quality, innovation, community, storytelling*); its guiding principles (*exceed customer experience; create valued experiences through business design*); and fit the culture of the brand by associating with key words (*imagination, wonder, magic, dreams, entertainment*), brought throughout the experience.

Case Study: *Starbucks*

Starbucks is an American coffee company and coffeehouse chain, founded in 1971 and currently operates 23,786 locations worldwide.

Understanding Howard Schultz, President and CEO

Schultz began his career in sales at Xerox and later worked as general manager for Swedish drip coffee maker manufacturer, Hamarplast.

It was there that he met the original founders of *Starbucks Coffee Company* in Seattle. Schultz kept in touch over the next year, expressing his interest in working for the company. A year later, he joined *Starbucks* as Director of Marketing.

It was a buying trip for *Starbucks* to Milan, Italy that opened Schultz' eyes to the cafe concept where they serve excellent espresso and provide meeting places and public squares for gathering.

Due to a disagreement on the strategy of *Starbucks*, Schultz left the company to pursue the cafe concept, opening *Il Giornale* cafes in Seattle. In 1988, the original founders of *Starbucks* decided to focus their efforts on *Peet's Coffee & Tea* and agreed to sell *Starbucks* to Schultz for $3.8 million USD.

Schultz renamed *Il Giornale* cafes to *Starbucks* and aggressively expanded its reach across the United States. Through Schultz's relentless persistence, perseverance and his focus on delivering a unique *Starbucks* experience to customers, the company has managed to achieve its vision to become the world's premier purveyor of the finest coffee in the world while maintaining a set of uncompromising principles as they have grown.

Understanding *Starbucks*, the Brand

Starbucks coffee is unlike other coffee brands. While focused on purveying the finest coffees, the brand is just as focused on other aspects of the experience that make it unique.

Starbucks' Foundational Elements

Vision
To establish Starbucks as the premier purveyor of the finest coffee in the world while maintaining our uncompromising principles while we grow.

Mission
To inspire and nurture the human spirit - one person, one cup and one neighborhood at a time
– September 2015

Brand Promise
Our promise: love it or let us know

Core Values
1. *Provide a great work environment and treat each other with respect and dignity*
2. *Embrace diversity as an essential component in the way we do business*
3. *Apply the highest standards of excellence to the purchasing, roasting, and fresh delivery of our coffee*
4. *Develop enthusiastically satisfied customers all the time*
5. *Contribute positively to our communities and our environment*
6. *Recognize that profitability is essential to our future success*

Guiding Principles[6]

1. *Creating a culture of warmth and belonging, where everyone is welcome.*
2. *Acting with courage, challenging the status quo and finding new ways to grow our company and each other.*
3. *Being present, connecting with transparency, dignity, and respect.*
4. *Delivering our very best in all we do, holding ourselves accountable for results.*

---

[6] Source:
http://www.slideshare.net/leadingresource/examples-of-company-core-values

Foundational Elements Analysis

Looking at the components that make up *Starbucks*' brand foundation, there is a clear spirit of helping each within the organization and outward facing with their audience. *Starbucks* has strong beliefs in making the world a better place through nurture and inspiration while staying true to the principles they have adopted.

Starbucks has a clear vision for itself and an understanding of how it will achieve its goals while staying true to its beliefs in applying the highest standards of excellence for their coffee, contributing to communities and the environment, while providing a great place to work and a culture that treats everyone with respect and dignity.

All of these values come through in the *Starbucks* experience, each and every time.

Founder's Words

Howard Schultz has been heavily focused on developing a rich culture that values diversity and respect, along with applying the highest levels of excellence, recognizing that profitability is essential to *Starbucks'* success.

This balance of values and ambitious goals align with Schultz' vision for *Starbucks'* future. Words that Schultz uses include "nurture," "home," and "inspiration."

Key Words

Further analyzing the brand foundation components, you can get a sense of the keywords that the *Starbucks* brand itself wants to be known for. Here is a short list:

- Premier purveyor
- Finest coffee
- World
- Principles
- Nurture
- Home
- Inspirational
- Natural
- Human Spirit
- Neighborhood
- Grow
- Natural

These words are not only associative to the *Starbucks* brand, but they are used in their messaging to guide the customer, step into their world.

Unpacking the *Starbucks'* Experience

Part of *Starbucks'* explosive growth has come from the strategy of maintaining approximately 80% of the total coffeehouses across the world. This allows tighter control over the coffeehouse experience, increasing consistency. Approximately 21% of *Starbucks* stores are licensed.

Physical Design Experience

Starbucks' coffeehouse interiors have continuously changed over the years, creating an inviting space that feels like a third home. To achieve this, *Starbucks* uses many natural materials and amplifies the experience with the five senses. Visually, soft lighting creates a relaxing environment and sets the mood as soon as you enter the cafe. Warm, earthy, organic materials are used, bringing *Starbucks'* mission and core values to life.

The aroma of coffee and baked goods waft throughout the coffeehouse while curated music express the artisanal hand-crafted drinks.

Together, *Starbucks* delivers an experience like no other. And they are able to consistently deliver their unique experience across nearly 25,000 coffeehouses around the world, staying true to their core values and principles from which they operate.

Figure 2: This sketch was inspired by a Starbucks coffeehouse in New Orleans, LA.

Digital Design Experience

In 2009, *Starbucks* rolled out a loyalty card program to reward its coffee drinkers. In 2010, *Starbucks* launched a mobile app that enhanced the experience. And in 2011, the brand introduced mobile payments.

Now, as of this writing in 2016, the *Starbucks* mobile app is one of the most successful loyalty and mobile payment systems in the world.

The app has continued to evolve and has enhanced the *Starbucks* experience further, showing the song playing overhead, providing directions, personalized menu options depending on the coffeehouse you are at, as well as allowing you to check your balance, reload your card, and order coffee through the app.

This has created a more personalized experience, fusing regular customers with the *Starbucks* brand, deepening the relationship. It has eliminated long lines, allowing *Starbucks* to increase the number of customers served in the same amount of time.

It has allowed customers to ensure they can customize their hand-crafted coffee without fear of the order being misheard, reducing variability and increasing brand trust.

This ties in with *Starbucks'* brand promise of *"love it or let us know."*

Chapter 6:

Putting it All Together

We've done it. We've gone through this journey together and now I pass the brand strategy pencil to you.

Now is the time to take action.

I've discussed and debunked the four biggest myths about branding and brand strategy. I've shared my unique approach to brand strategy, which focuses on the operations and foundational components of an organization in order to allow the internal brand to come to the surface.

We took a deep dive into the five foundational elements of unshakable brands. We dissected, analyzed, and determined best practices for developing each element. We then focused on how to bring those qualities and values to life by delivering unique and immersive brand experiences.

We've covered a lot. *And we're just scratching the surface!*

It is now up to you to complete each of the foundational elements for your organization. These foundational elements will help secure your brand, give it deeper meaning and provide a means to connect with your ideal audience.

So what are you waiting for? Your business isn't going to brand itself.

Your clients are waiting to be amazed.

> To get your free ***GROUNDWORK* Worksheet**, visit www.brandedworld.co/gw

About the Author

Benjamin Warsinske is a thought leader on brand architecture and strategy. Fueled by imagination and a desire to help organizations deliver exceptional experiences, he consults and trains clients on how to develop cohesive brands and compelling brand experiences.

Benjamin can help your brand become *unshakable* via his brand strategy firm, *BrandedWorld.co, Inc.* For more information, please visit www.BrandedWorld.co.

About BrandedWorld.co, Inc.

BrandedWorld.co is a brand strategy firm headquartered in Chicago, Illinois.

Our mission is to revolutionize fragmented, transactional businesses into unshakable brands delivering exceptional experiences.

We live and breathe our core values, which guide us in our work: aloha, integrity, quality, and empowerment.

We provide live on-site workshops and on demand training through our innovative online Academy platform.

To learn more about the **BrandedWorld Academy** and how to become a member, visit www.brandedworld.co/academy.

Acknowledgements

Many people have encouraged me and have helped me to bring **GroundWork** to you, and have contributed to the maturing of this book and body of work. To all of those who have had listened to my research conclusions, offered perspective, and have read portions of this book as it was being written, thank you for your gracious help and responses.

To friends, colleagues, and business partners, both online and off, thank you for your support with this work. I am thankful to have you in my circle and appreciate the encouragement you provide to keep going in order to help others. I'm just getting started and am excited for what is around the corner.

To my family and extended family, thank you for your ongoing support, love, and cheerleading every step of the way. While the path has not always been clear, knowing that I have your support helps me keep pushing forward towards realizing my dream. Thank you.

And to Jacqueleen – wife and amazing partner – I am incredibly grateful to you and all that you have done to help me bring this book to life. For your tireless nights of editing, listening, and continuous encouragement, I cannot begin to thank you enough. You have been an incredible companion, partner, friend, and wife. Thank you.

Suggested Reading & References

The following books and resources influenced the writing of this book. For additional resources, please visit www.BrandedWorld.co.

Books

Cialdini, Robert B. *Influence: The Psychology of Persuasion*. New York, NY: Collins Business, 2007.

Dweck, Carol S. *Mindset*. New York, NY: Random House, Inc., 2006.

Gobe, Marc. *Emotional Branding: The New Paradigm for Connecting Brands to People*. New York, NY: Allworth Press, 2009.

Klaff, Oren. *Pitch Anything*. New York, NY: McGraw-Hill, 2011.

Lindstrom, Martin. *Buyology*. New York, NY: DoubleDay, 2008.

Taylor, William C. and Labarre, Polly. *Mavericks at Work*. New York, NY: HarperCollins Publishers, 2006.

Weinberg, Mike. *New Sales. Simplified.* New York, NY: American Management Association, 2013.

Studies & Reports

"Brand Intimacy 2015 Report." *MBLM*. MBLM. Web 01 Nov. 2016
http://mblm.com/brandintimacy/report.

"Millennial Survey 2016." *Deloitte.* Deloitte Touche Tohmatsu Limited, 15 June 2016. Web. 10 Oct 2016.
https://www2.deloitte.com/global/en/pages/about-deloitte/articles/millennialsurvey.html.